VIRTUAL MENACE

THE LITTLE BOOK OF CYBER SCAMS

PEER TEHLEEL MANZOOR

CONTENTS

GDPR

INTRODUCTION

Peer Tehleel Manzoor is pleased to bring his 5th Tech book of Cyber Scams Version

This book has been specifically designed to offer advice relevant to both individuals and also Small and Medium Enterprises (SMEs) on staying safe in the cyber world. With day to day life being increasingly tied to the internet, this book aims to highlight some of the dangers you might face, as well as offer advice on how to protect yourself.

For Business Perspective

SMEs can be found everywhere: on the high street, industrial estates, online and at home, and they are vital to the overall success of the British economy. Often, with limited resources and turbulent economic conditions, SMEs typically prioritize innovation and growth over due diligence, online security and risk mitigation. These issues can often be seen as expensive, burdensome and time consuming business practices. It is important though that these areas are acknowledged and reviewed and that companies are aware of the risks their businesses face from cyber criminals.

Protect Yourself

Whether we are an individual or a business, we all rely on the internet. We buy and sell on it, speak to our friends, contact our customers, use it for logistical support or simply for entertainment. But with all the opportunities it brings, it is important to remember the risks.

Every day thousands of computer systems all over the world are attacked. There are criminals who take advantage of the anonymity of the online world to deceive, hack and steal if the opportunity arises. If an attack is successful, it could have a significant effect on you. As an individual, you could have criminals access your online banking, or even lose access to your family photos, unless you pay them a ransom. This doesn't mean you shouldn't use the internet. Implementing a few, simple, security processes and making your friends and family, or your staff aware of the threats, can make a significant difference to your chances of becoming the victim of a cyber criminal.

This book aims to identify common types of cyber crime and the ways you can protect yourself from them. It is not an exhaustive list, in what is an ever-changing landscape, but by following the advice given you can increase your personal knowledge and protection.

CYBER CRIME TYPES

When talking about cyber crime, it is useful to distinguish between the two different categories.

Cyber-dependent

Cyber-dependent crimes (or 'pure' cyber crimes) are offences that can only be committed using a computer, computer networks or other form of information communications technology (ICT). This include the spread of viruses or other malware, hacking and distributed denial of service (DDoS) attacks. All of these will be explained later in this book. All cyber- dependent crimes are in violation of the Computer Misuse Act 1990.

If a device or network is connected to the internet, it can be attacked by a cyber criminal. If they manage to gain access, they can steal your data, monitor what you're doing or even take control. In addition, they can use data gathered this way to commit further offences like accessing online bank accounts, or committing fraud.

Cyber-enabled

Cyber-enabled crimes are traditional crimes, such as fraud, which can be increased in their scale or reach through the use of computers, or other ICT devices (i.e. mobile phones or computer networks).

According to Action Fraud, it is estimated that at least 84% of fraud reported nationally is cyber enabled. This is because computers allow criminals to target a much wider audience for their frauds, with several fraud types being more common than others. Some are outlined in this book, and others are detailed in the Little Book of Big Scams, also published by the Metropolitan Police.

CYBER-DEPENDENT: HACKING

Hacking occurs when a criminal manages to gain unauthorized access to a computer system. There are a number of ways in which computer systems can be hacked.

Password attacks

The criminal will use computer programs that attempt to guess passwords to allow access to a system. The program will generate passwords based on pre-defined terms and will then use these passwords to try and break into the system. Given enough time, and computing power, most passwords can be cracked. This can be made easier by the criminal successfully investigating the potential victim via data leakage (see page 20) and adding more of the victim's personal information to their password cracking program.

Application attacks

This Involves targeting weaknesses in the computer system's applications or programs. Often programs or software will have vulnerabilities that can be exploited to allow security to be breached.

HOW TO PROTECT YOURSELF FROM HACKING

Use a firewall

A firewall is designed to protect one computer network from another. They are used between areas of high and low trust, like a private network and the internet. Firewalls offer protection by controlling traffic entering and leaving a network. The firewall does this using a set of filters or rules that are set by the user to allow or block particular types of traffic.

Most personal computer operating systems come with a software firewall installed and turned on. However, this is always worth checking.

Keep software updated

It is important to make sure any software on your computer is kept up to date as its designers are constantly improving. It as new vulnerabilities are discovered. This is done by downloading updates or 'patches' from the software developer. It is also important to make sure that up to date software is used as older software may be redundant and not have updated support. This means that any new vulnerabilities found by cyber criminals will not be fixed, leaving the software vulnerable to attack. This is especially true for operating systems.

Have strong passwords

Often IT system security is breached because a default password on software or hardware has not been changed. It is important that all default passwords are changed as soon as practicable.There are a number of general rules regarding passwords that will make them more secure:

Make a password as long as possible, the more characters it has the harder it is to crack.

Use different types of characters including numbers, symbols and punctuation marks.

Try not to include only dictionary words in your password as this makes them easier to crack.

Try to avoid personal names, like family, pets or sports teams.

Use different passwords for different accounts, especially for your email address. This way, if one password is compromised then at least only one account can be hacked

Check to see if your email address or password has been leaked in a previous data breach on https://haveibeenpwned.com

This way, a criminal needs both factors (in this example, your password and your phone) to gain access to your accounts or systems.

For further information, and help on Multi Factor Authentication, check http://twofactorauth.org or www.turnon2fa.com

CYBER-DEPENDENT: DDoS

A Distributed Denial of Service (DDoS) attack is an attempt to make an internet based service, such as a website, unavailable by overwhelming it with data traffic. Usually this is achieved by sending a flood of simultaneous requests to a server, which causes the server to crash as it struggles to respond to more requests than it can handle. These types of attacks are frequently carried out against websites, usually using a network of remotely controlled computers sometimes referred to as a botnet. The computers that are part of the botnet have usually been infected with malicious software (see page 16) allowing the cyber criminals the ability to direct traffic at the victim's server.

DDoS attacks in themselves do not cause damage to your systems. When the attack stops, your server and attached services should return to normal. Loss of systems though, for whatever time frame, can lead to loss of sales or reputational damage.

DDoS attacks can also be used as a smokescreen to camouflage or draw attention away from other illegal activity an attacker might be committing against a company's systems, such as stealing data from the network.

Most victims of DDoS attacks are high profile organizations such as multinationals, government agencies, banks and other financial institutions.

However, no organization is immune and it is important to be aware that this type of attack can happen.

DDoS extortion

DDoS extortion involves a cyber criminal contacting a business and threatening to subject them to a DDoS attack if they do not pay them a sum of money. These threats are usually made via email and request that funds are paid by the company via a hard to trace route such as cryptocurrency.

HOW TO PROTECT YOURSELF FROM DDoS

Knowing the signs of an active attack Identifying that a DDoS attack is occurring allows for mitigation to be implemented at the earliest opportunity.

The following symptoms could indicate a DDoS attack on your network:

Unusually slow network performance (opening files or accessing websites)

Unavailability of a particular website Inability to access any website

A dramatic increase in the number of spam emails received

If an active attack is occurring, you should make contact with your internet service provider, as well as your web host, to make them aware. You should also contact law enforcement.

Invest in DDoS mitigation

There are numerous different DDoS mitigation applications available from various suppliers. These work by analyzing data traffic and identifying rogue traffic, which is then not allowed to reach the target server.

DDoS extortion

If you are the victim of DDoS extortion do not pay any demands. Retain any emails sent by the cyber criminal and report the incident directly to law enforcement

SOCIAL ENGINEERING – HACKING THE HUMAN

Social Engineering is defined as "The clever manipulation of the natural human tendency to trust." It's easier to trick you into opening an infected email than it is to hack into your system. Due to this, social engineering has become much more prominent, and cyber criminals are trying more diverse ways to get people to undertake tasks, provide information or hand over money using these techniques.

Types of social engineering

Phishing

Often cyber criminals will send emails pretending to be someone else, for example a bank, online auction site or government department. The aim of the email is to install malware or obtain login credentials. Due to the nature of the internet, they can send out the same email to countless recipients at the same time. According

to studies done by ISACA, 90% of cyber breaches started with phishing emails. By making the email appear to be from a legitimate source, the receiver is more likely to reply or take the action requested in the email.

Software is available that can alter, or "spoof" an email address in the sender line of an email. This means that when you look at the email, it appears to have been sent from someone else.The email may also be sent from an email address that is similar to the genuine sender. Without taking time to check the authenticity of the sender's address, the receiver may believe the email is from a genuine source.

The phishing email, for example, could request log on details for internet banking websites, which look identical to real ones. This may be under the guise of security questions to confirm the receiver's identity. Once inputted, these details can be harvested by the cyber criminal and can be used to steal from online bank accounts or make purchases from online retailers.

Phishing emails may also contain malicious software in attachments that you are directed to open. The cyber criminal may send tens, or hundreds, of thousands of the same phishing email to different email addresses hoping that a small percentage of recipients will reply. It can only take one response with the right information for a cyber criminal to have the opportunity of making thousands of pounds.

Smishing

Smishing is the SMS equivalent to phishing, so the malicious message appears on your phone as a text. Criminals can disguise their phone number to make it look like it's from a reputable source and try to convince you to click on an attached link. When received, these messages can appear in the same text thread as genuine messages.

Spear phishing

Spear phishing is a more direct form of phishing where the email will target a specific person. Often, the 'sender' is shown as a person the receiver knows, for example a work colleague, a more senior employee or someone from the company's IT department.

The email may also contain other information about the receiver that has been obtained from the internet such as universities attended or restaurants visited. This information is known as data leakage and can make the email seem more genuine.

HOW TO PROTECT YOURSELF FROM SOCIAL ENGINEERING ATTACKS

The best defense against social engineering attacks is knowledge, whether this is individually, or as staff education and awareness training. By making people aware of the issue, they will be able to combat it.

How to check the sender email address on an email.

Hovering the mouse cursor over the email address shown in the sender box should show the email address the email has actually come from. Be aware though, this function can be overridden. Also, check that the email address shown is a genuine email address and has not been spelt incorrectly

Often phishing emails will be sent from an email account similar to a genuine company email address rather than a genuine corporate account This gives the impression that the email has come from a legitimate sender, as the corporate name is shown in the sender email address.

Each email platform will have ways in which the actual sender of the email can be found. An internet search will help you find the way for your own specific email platform.

What to do if a request is made to provide bank details, personal information or log-in details.

If a request for this type of information is made, then it should be verified by making contact with the organization. Don't reply to, or use any of the contact details from the email, instead use already established details. If you have no contact details already, contact the organization using details sourced from an internet search

In addition, neither banks, nor police will ever ask for passwords, bank cards or PIN codes, and will certainly never ask you to withdraw or transfer money.

Never login to any type of account (shopping, social media, financial, etc.) by clicking on a link you've received in a text or email. Always go to your browser independently, and use your usual links.

PAYMENT FRAUD

Payment fraud is a specific type of cyber enabled fraud which targets businesses with the intention of getting them to transfer money to a bank account operated by the cyber criminal. Payment fraud is becoming one of the most prolific frauds targeting businesses, and so deserves a special mention.

There are two main types of payment fraud, CEO fraud and Mandate Fraud. Both are usually targeted at staff within a company's accounts department and use spoofed sender email addresses. CEO fraud involves an email that claims to be from a senior member of staff within a company such as a CEO (Chief Executive Officer). The email will ask the receiver to make a payment or transfer funds for an ongoing or new business transaction.Often the payment request is marked as urgent and pressure is applied to the receiver to make the payment as soon as possible. Mandate fraud involves an email which appears to come from a known supplier. The email will request that future payments for products or services are made to a new bank account and give a reason for the account change. In each instance, the new account will be under the control of the cyber criminal and any funds paid in to it will be lost.

HOW TO PROTECT YOURSELF FROM PAYMENT FRAUD

If an email is received requesting a change of bank details on an account or a one off payment, verify this by making direct contact with the organization or person requesting the change using established contact details. Don't be pressurized by any email, or follow up phone call, as this may be the criminal. Always double check.

Case study

The Finance Director of a small HR company received an email they believed was from the company's CEO as their email address was shown in the sender box of the email. The email directed the Finance Director to make a payment in to a bank account shown on the email. Believing the request was genuine the Finance director transferred £30,000

to the account. The Finance Director was contacted by the company's bank regarding the transaction, and its authenticity, and confirmed to the bank it was a genuine transaction. It was later discovered that the request was fraudulent and the funds that had been transferred could not be recovered.

Police identified that both the CEO's and Finance Director's business email addresses were shown on the company's website therefore greatly

assisting the cyber criminal in creating the spear phishing email. It was also found that by hovering over the email address on the email sent by the criminal the true sender email address could be seen.

MALWARE

The term malware refers to malicious software. This is software that is designed to gain unauthorized access to computers or other connected devices, and disrupt their normal operation or gather information from them.

Malware can infect a computer or network from a number of sources including:

Contaminated email attachments Visiting infected websites, eitherdirectly or via links embedded within emails or social media posts

From corrupt files stored on external devices such as memory sticks, DVDs, CDs or cameras that are plugged in to a network

Common types of malware

Spyware

Spyware is designed to steal information about your activity on a computer or other device. Spyware can perform a number of functions including recording screen shots or logging keystrokes.This enables the criminal to harvest data that has been input into a computer in order to use it themselves, such as internet banking passwords. Remote Access Trojans (RATs) are a type of spyware which allows a cyber criminal to remotely connect to infected devices and control them as if they were the authorized user.

Ransomware

Ransomware is a form of malware that enables cyber criminals to remotely lock down files on a computer or device. This means that the operator cannot access the locked files on the computer making them unusable. Once the files have been locked the criminal will make contact with the victim and offer to unlock them for a fee, the 'ransom'. Payment is usually requested via a hard to trace route such as cryptocurrency

Virus/Worm

Viruses and worms infect host systems and then spread to infect others. Once on a system, viruses and worms insert copies of themselves into programs, files, and drives. They then have the ability to spread onto other computers using the network the first infected device is attached to. Worms and viruses can also carry additional "payloads" designed to perform harmful activity on their hosts. This type of malware can cause damage that rapidly becomes widespread. Worms can enable attackers to create a network of hijacked machines (sometimes referred to as a botnet) which can be used in a distributed denial-of-service (DDoS) attack

HOW TO PROTECT YOURSELF FROM MALWARE

Use antivirus software

Install this software on all your applicable devices. This includes most smartphones, computers and servers. It will monitor for malware within the device's memory, processes and storage and alert you if any is found. Most antivirus software can remove malicious software it has detected and repair damage it may have caused. It is important to make sure any antivirus software is kept up to date as its designers are constantly improving the software as new malware programs are discovered. This is done by downloading updates or 'patches' from the software provider.

Use a firewall.

Back up your data regularly

Make regular backups of important work and data to a separate device such as a portable hard drive, and check that backups have been successful. If possible, backups should be encrypted and stored in a safe place such as a fireproof safe.

If your computer is infected by malware, such as ransomware, it can then be restored using the backup and any locked or lost data can be restored. Ideally, you should backup data to two separate locations, only one of which should be in the cloud Implement device control Prevent malware from infecting computers by restricting what devices can be connected to them such as USB drives and smartphones. These can carry malware which can transfer to the host computer when they are plugged in to it. Don't connect any unknown or untrusted device to your systems Don't follow links or open attachments in emails unless from a trusted source Opening links and attachments in emails may allow malicious software to be downloaded onto your system or device. Malware can be concealed in email attachments or downloaded from a malicious webpage. If you receive an email from an unknown source, or it's a trusted source, but the email isn't like their usual email, don't click on any link without checking first.

DATA LEAKAGE

The information you post online can be a treasure trove for a cyber criminal. Social media sites are used by millions of people every day, and many people have online profiles where a significant amount of information is detailed about them, their employment and their education.

In the same way a criminal may see you are on holiday from a social media post and burglarize your house, a cyber criminal may use a work contact email address or details of a conference you are attending, which you have posted online, to assist in a cyber attack against you.

It is very easy for a cyber criminal to create a spear phishing email from the information that can be found online using simple searches via a search engine. This is called 'open source information' and is available on the internet without requiring access to secure areas on any website

For example, a simple tweet about a visit to a restaurant could be used to create a spear phishing email that appears to come from the restaurant. This email may offer you the opportunity to enter a competition or claim a discount on your next visit by completing a form attached to the email. This form may contain malicious software and on opening it the malware can spread on to your computer.

HOW TO PROTECT YOURSELF FROM DATA LEAKAGE

Be wary of what you post online. Does the information have to be in the public domain?

Know what information can be found about you online Complete a simple open source internet search to see what data is available about you. There may be information posted

by others that you are not aware of, or information you didn't know was posted in the public domain.

Separate business information from personal information and who can see which

Don't have personal contact details on business websites and vice versa.

Keep work and personal life separate.

Have high security settings on social media sites

Don't let everyone see everything. Make sure that personal information and details you only want friends or colleagues to see are kept private by using the security settings on social media sites. Set them to ensure that only the people you want to see your information can see it, and encourage your friends and family to do the same. In addition, be wary of people that want to follow or friend you. Consider what interest they may have in you and whether they are suitable to see personal information about you.

WI-FI HOTSPOTS

Publicly available Wi-Fi connections or 'hot spots' can be useful for accessing the internet when you are not at home or your workplace.

Not all Wi-Fi connections are secure though, and there are ways in which they can be used by cyber criminal to intercept your data.

Sniffing

Sniffing is a technique whereby the cyber criminal can connect to the same Wi-Fi network as you, and see any data you send. By doing this they can steal passwords, login details and sensitive information and then either use it to commit offences against you, or sell

it on to another party. Even if you are not typing login credentials into your device every time you open an app on a phone, such as an email or social media application, login details are sent across the network and can be intercepted.

Evil Access Points

Alternatively, cyber criminals can set up their own public Wi-Fi hotspots in an attempt to get you to connect to them. First they connect their computer to the internet, then they imitate a Wi-Fi connection, often calling it something like 'free_wifi' or 'coffee_shop_wifi'. Once you connect to the hot spot you are effectively connecting to the criminal's computer and they can capture any data you are sending.

Protect yourself

Use a Virtual Private Network (VPN) when accessing public Wi-Fi connections. By using a VPN all your data will be encrypted as it's transferred over the network so that if it's intercepted by anyone, they won't be able to read it.

VPNs can be downloaded onto phones and computers as an app.

Don't do anything on public Wi-Fi that you wouldn't want a cyber criminal to see, such as online banking, accessing company emails or anything that requires you to enter a username or password.

If you are unsure as to whether a Wi-Fi hotspot connection is secure do not use it and use your 3G or 4G data connection to access the internet instead. Data passed over 3G and 4G is encrypted.

BUSINESS RISKS

What is at risk?

Businesses are even more likely to be targeted by cyber criminals. Your money, your reputation, your data, your IT equipment and IT based services such as websites and payment systems are all at risk.

Data can take many forms and includes client lists, payment information, product details and private company information. There can be a risk to data wherever it is stored whether this is on company IT systems and devices or in the cloud. An IT breach can be costly both in the cost to fix it and reputational damage. A breach could also lead to funds being stolen or fraudulently transferred from company bank accounts. A loss of data

may also incur a significant fine from the Information Commissioner's Office.

Who could pose a threat?

Criminals looking to steal from you – whether this is data or money. They may also wish to disrupt your systems so your business cannot function normally.

Competitors wanting to obtain your private company data or wanting to disrupt your operations.

Your own staff. Your employees may have access to a significant amount of data and information held by your company. Disgruntled employees may steal this with the intention of passing it to competitors or to the highest bidder. Staff may also be tricked or 'socially engineered' in to providing data they should not have to a cyber criminal.

Hackers want to show off their skills and prove to others that they can breach your security.

How to protect your business

SMEs face a particular difficulty in balancing their cyber prevention activities with the resources they have available in both money and time.

It is important that SME's do not put profitability at risk by implementing unnecessary and expensive 'gold standard' cyber control systems. Instead, a basic, pragmatic and practical approach is best.

Understand where your business is most at risk of cyber attack.

Conduct a review of your business functions and processes and consider how a cyber criminal may seek to exploit any weakness. This review should include both IT infrastructure and staff awareness and training.

Develop systems and processes to reduce these risks.

Focus on closing gaps that could be targeted by a cyber criminal and cause the greatest amount of damage to your business.

Create a cyber crime prevention culture within your business.

Train staff on how to spot cyber crime and what to do once identified. Cyber prevention training should not be a one-off activity and staff should be regularly updated in this area. All staff should be made aware of company cyber crime prevention policies and procedures.

Have contingency plans in place and test them regularly.

Being the victim of cyber crime can lead to a chain of events that can be incredibly disruptive, damaging and costly to your business. It is important that the relevant people are aware of their roles and responsibilities if a cyber crime is identified. Having effective plans in place will help your business recover as quickly as possible. Regularly review your functions and processes. Ensure that cybercrime mitigation is relevant and effective, and that processes are adhered to. Where new security issues are identified implement new or improved procedures/ functions to mitigate these problems. Proportionality is key. Make sure the systems and processes you implement are appropriate to your business type and size. Keep your software up to date. Businesses especially need to ensure that the various software used in running their business is kept current to ensure that all vulnerabilities are closed as soon as they are found. As part of the cyber crime prevention culture, encourage your staff to do the same on their personal devices.

GDPR

The European General Data Protection Regulation (GDPR) came in to force on May 25th 2018 and bought into effect a set of rules that anyone processing personal data must abide by. Personal data is information that relates to an identified or identifiable individual. This means if you can identify an individual directly from the information you are processing, then that information may be personal data. Data subjects now have more rights as to how their data can be used. This non- exhaustive list includes the right to be informed, to object, to rectify and to erase with regards to any data held about them. The GDPR also introduces a duty on an organization to report certain types of personal data breaches to the relevant supervisory authority. They must do this within 72 hours of becoming aware of the breach, where feasible. In addition, if the breach is likely to result in a high risk of adversely affecting individuals' rights and freedoms, they must also inform those individuals without undue delay. If you fail to do so, you can be fined up to 2% of global turnover or €10m. To ensure your organization is GDPR compliant, it is highly recommended that you consult the Information Commissioner's Office's website at https://ico.org.uk/.

THE FUTURE

The internet has opened a world of opportunity to business and consumers. It has sped up transactions, simplified processes and created a more convenient interface between businesses and customers. Many small businesses are run using only a laptop from a kitchen table. Technology will continue to improve, but what effect will this have on security?

The Internet of Things – IoT

With the increase in the number of internet connected devices, such as cars, TVs and fridges, it hasn't taken long for cyber criminals to identify how to exploit them in order to commit cyber crime.One of the ways they do this, is to utilise the internet connection of IoT devices to launch DDoS attacks (see page 8). To help counteract this, always check the security settings of any IoT device that you purchase, and make sure that you change any default passwords.

Escalation of cyber extortion

We expect to see more ransomware and large ransom demands made against victims, especially when a large business is threatened. As well as using more complex malware to encrypt files we also expect to see an increase in the number of cyber extortion groups and methods of attack. Cyber criminals are already demanding ransoms to halt DDoS attacks, or are approaching businesses with demands for cash after stealing critical data from company networks.

GLOSSARY

Botnet

A collection of infected computers which can be remotely controlled by a cyber criminal.

Brute force attack

The use of computer programs to try and identify the password allowing unauthorized access to a system.

Cloud computing

The term for a company or individual using a third party company to store their data, applications and files and access them through this company's system, rather than storing all their information on their own servers. Examples include iCloud, Amazon Web Services, Dropbox and Google drive.

Cookies

Files held on your computer containing information about your website usage.

Data loss

The accidental loss of data, not its theft.

Data theft

The deliberate theft of data.

Data leakage

When information about a person or business is published online. This information may be used to construct spear phishing emails.

Distributed Denial of Service attack (DDoS)

An attack launched on a system by a network of computers, called a Botnet, which causes disruption to a computer or website.

Email malware distribution Malware which is delivered via an attachment in an email.

Exploits

These are designed to take advantage of a flaw or vulnerability in a computer system, typically for malicious purposes such as installing malware.

Hacktivism

This is hacking that takes places for political or social purposes.

Keylogging

This involves the logging of keystrokes on a compromised computer or device.

Malware

This is malicious software which includes spyware, Trojans, viruses and worms.

Patches

These are fixes for vulnerabilities found in software, operating systems or applications.

Phishing emails

This is the process of tricking recipients into revealing sensitive information via the sending of fraudulent emails.

Ransomware

This is a type of malware that denies you access to your files or computer until a ransom is paid.

Social Engineering

This refers to the manipulation of victims into disclosing information or completing a task they would not usually do.

Spear phishing

This is targeted phishing often using spoofed email addresses and containing information found from 'data leakage' to add legitimacy to its content.

Spoofing

Email spoofing is when the sender email address is falsified to assist in social engineering. Software available online is used to hide the true sender of an email.

Spyware

This is malicious software that allows cyber criminals to obtain private information without a user's knowledge. It may record keystrokes or which websites have been visited and pass this information to the cyber criminal.

Contents

Printed by Libri Plureos GmbH in Hamburg,
Germany